Richard Salter Storrs

The Work of Winning Souls

Richard Salter Storrs

The Work of Winning Souls

ISBN/EAN: 9783337340735

Printed in Europe, USA, Canada, Australia, Japan

Cover: Foto ©Lupo / pixelio.de

More available books at **www.hansebooks.com**

1. THE WORK OF WINNING SOULS, A WISE ONE:

AND

2. THE SPIRITUAL HELP WHICH A CHURCH GIVES TO ITS MINISTER.

TWO SERMONS

PREACHED IN

The Church of the Pilgrims,

BROOKLYN, N. Y.,

November 18, 1866,

ON THE COMPLETION OF

Twenty Years of Pastoral Service;

BY RICHARD S. STORRS. JR., D. D.,

Printed by Request.

BROOKLYN:
"THE UNION" STEAM PRESSES, NO. 10 FRONT STREET.

1866.

NOTE.

For the preservation of the first of the following discourses, which was delivered extemporaneously, I am almost wholly indebted to the notes of the Reporter.

Neither this, nor that which follows it, was prepared with any reference to its publication through the press. But as a desire for such publication has been expressed by those who heard the sermons, I am happy to have it gratified,—particularly as it gives me the opportunity to put on record, in this permanent form, my most grateful and affectionate regard for the Church and Congregation to which it has so long been my privilege to minister, in the hope and service of the Gospel.

R. S. STORRS, Jr.

Brooklyn, Nov. 24, 1866.

MORNING SERMON.

Proverbs, 11 : 30, (Last Clause.)

"AND HE THAT WINNETH SOULS IS WISE."

ONE cannot but be impressed, in his observation of human affairs, as these go on in society around him, with the transientness which belongs to many of the enterprises in which men are engaged, and to which their hearts are most eagerly given. The law of change is alone unchangeable. Mutation, precariousness, pertain to everything which we meet in the world; to every institution which we establish, that is not philanthrophic or religious in its relations; to every enterprise which we set on foot, that has not a moral end to serve.

A man accumulates a splendid property, by skill, by industry, by enterprise and economy. It looks solid and stately, when he has gained it; and he expects it to continue while he lives, to be admired by others, to be enjoyed by himself, and to minister to his household comfort and cheer. But we know that sudden commercial disaster may sweep against it with irresistible energy, may break it in pieces, and scatter the glittering fragments of it across the land. And we know that even if no such commercial disaster comes, Death will ere long take him away from it, and that it will pass inevitably then into other hands, to be dispersed where his will can no longer control, where even his mind can no more follow, its successive distributions.

Or one builds a stately and ornamented house, in which to dwell, hoping to abide there himself while he lives, and to have his children abide there after him, when he has gone from these scenes of time. But the house to which he has given so much, of time, of thought, of the outlay of money, sometimes falls while he lives, before the changing enterprise of the city. The pleasant street in which it was built—filled with residences at the time it was built—becomes a street for busy traffic; and the house, so stately and splendid in its season, is leveled with the dust to make room for commercial structures, or is so changed for other uses, that he who built would fail to recognize it. And even if no such change takes place, it crumbles after a while; and when a few years have passed over his grave, its very stones, though outlasting himself, will have turned into dust, its solid timbers will have rotted.

So when one suggests a new theory in science, and publishes that in volumes to the world: a great impression may be made by it for the time on the minds of thoughtful and studious men. But it is singular to see how, with the rarest possible exceptions, within a few years the theory that looked plausible and satisfactory at the outset, has ceased to hold in allegiance to itself the minds of its students, and they have passed on, better instructed by other theories, to the larger view of the ampler system of which it showed but a partial conception. Or another devotes himself to the establishment of some special policy in the State, which seems to him to be right in itself, and for the advantage and interest of the State, in whose welfare and progress he is concerned. And after a little, when another generation has come upon the stage, and other questions have grown prominent and paramount, the policy to which he devoted so much of labor, of time, and of political skill, is found to have been wholly removed from the sphere of men's action and thought. It has simply passed away from their view, silently as the morning cloud; and the questions around which the minds of citizens surged and wrought so vehemently aforetime, have ceased to be questions appealing to them; the policy which the statesman sought so earnestly to develope and establish, is now a mere matter of historical interest, in which only the curious student of the Past finds any attraction.

So, everywhere, change is written on all the enterprises which men inaugurate, and all the establishments which they seek to build. And the question rises with a new emphasis: Is there any work which, when done, will remain? Is there anything which exists on the earth so substantial, and so enduring, that an effect produced upon it will stand, abiding and permanent as itself? And the answer is suggested by the words of the text: "He that winneth souls is wise." The personal soul is the one thing which continuously and immortally lives; which outlasts the body; which lives when the stately house has fallen, and the splendid fortune has been scattered; which lives when the theory that once was accepted has been surpassed and forgotten, and the policy of the statesman has passed from men's sight; which outlasts even the world itself, and the stars in heaven, on which the earth is poised and hangs; which lives while God himself continues, and while his government continues to be exercised over intelligent moral beings. And he who devotes himself to accomplishing a work upon this personal human soul—that shall be for its essential welfare—undertakes a work that must be enduring and not brief; a work that must abide in its fruits when all the precarious enterprises of man, whereby he is surrounded, shall have come to their gradual or sudden termination.

To make more obvious the permanence and the greatness of this spiritual work, observe what it is which is implied in the welfare—the ultimate, enduring, and consummate welfare—of the soul, as it exists to-day and here, in you and me. There are four things implied in this, each of which we may briefly notice.

The first is: THE RECONCILIATION OF THAT SOUL WITH GOD, ITS AUTHOR, AND MORAL GOVERNOR; the reconciliation of it with Him, through faith in Christ and repentance from sin.

There is in every human heart a consciousness, more or less distinct, but central always as its own life, of alienation from God. This does not come out to any vivid exhibition in the ordinary run of human affairs, and the common experiences through which men pass. But it comes to even such an exhibition now and then —as when one contemplates Death, for example, as standing immediately before himself; that Death whose secret of terror is that by it the spirit is dislodged from the body, and is made to enter the presence of God, and to come for its judgment to his tribunal. In the instant expectation of this, one becomes aware, if he was not before, that the soul in himself is divorced from God. It shrinks from entering the presence of the Infinite. And there is the patent and unanswerable proof of its inner moral alienation from him. For there could be no other privilege so grand, no other opportunity so supreme, to the created human spirit, as this of entering the presence of its Creator, if it were essentially in harmony with him.

How we value the privilege that comes with the

occasional opportunity of converse with some imperial human mind, or some all-accomplished human scholar! the privilege that comes with the opportunity of standing in personal communion for a little with a mind characterized by extraordinary genius, whose words are as beams of irradiating light, to illumine and inspire our duller intellect! But surely there is no privilege of this kind for an instant to be compared with, which does not differ infinitely from, the privilege of standing in the presence of God, whose eternal mind has planned and built the universe itself, and from whom we must, as intelligent beings, derive a constant and glorious inspiration, through every touch of his soul upon ours! When then men shrink from entering his presence, they show the consciousness, living within them, of a central alienation from him; and so they show, without thinking of it perhaps, that the first and deepest want of their soul is this of reconciliation with him.

There can be no real welfare for man until this in some way has been accomplished. It matters not what properties we accumulate, or what influence and power we wield in society. It matters not what delightful circumstances, and social relations, we gather around ourselves on the earth; what ships, sailing upon the ocean, own us as masters; what railroads, sweeping across the continent, run on our errands and carry our goods, to every point; or what other appliances and mechanisms of art, furnished by genius, we can command to do our bidding. It matters not at all what we may gain, and hold, and enjoy, of this world's wealth. There is no real prosperity possible to him whose soul is not reconciled to God,—so that he has ceased to be afraid of Death; so that Death is now full to him, not of threat and not of terror, but of precious invitation; so that his immortality is secure, and is certain to be glorious, through the harmony of his spirit with that of Him who made and who will judge him.

I put it to you as reasonable men, and reasonable women: there is no essential prosperity possible to the immortal soul in man, until it has thus become reconciled to God! You may be walking in the show and in the reality of wealth; you may be rejoicing in all the experience of pleasure in the world—delighting yourselves in the charms of art, in the beauties of nature, in the manifold joys of friendship and society, feasting your minds on the luxuries of literature, gathering pleasure and culture to yourselves from every quarter, and every source—and you are after all, at the centre and essentially, an unprosperous man, an unsuccessful, imperiled woman, until, by faith in the Lord Jesus Christ, you are reünited in spirit unto God! You cannot think of him as he is, and of yourselves as his rational creatures, without feeling this. There is *no* real welfare, till that is secured. The stellar universe, compressed into one bright circlet of gems, and worn to-day upon your forehead, could not make one of you tranquil or rich until you were conscious of this attainment.

And Christ has come to bring the offer, and open the way, of such a reconciliation to God; to put the means of it into our hands; to shed abroad the joy that comes with it, through our disturbed and anxious hearts. And he who "winneth souls" to Christ, secures for them this first element of their welfare.

But then, beyond this, it is necessary, secondly, that there be a DEVELOPMENT AND CULTURE IN US OF THE GOD-LIKE CHARACTER, in order to the true well-being of the soul; such a development and culture of this character as will naturally be based upon this reconciliation with God, through faith in His Son. And he who works on the soul for its good contributes also, and equally, to this.

To know what such a character is, we have first to know the character of Christ, as it was exhibited in his life on the earth. We do not find it fully revealed to us anywhere else. You point me to the universe around me, and above, and I admire the wisdom that has planned it, the might that has established it, and the will that carries it forward in its sweep, without a single jar or break, from age to age. But I see nothing in all this universe of that tender and intimate sympathy with man—in the feebleness, the suffering, and the peril he experiences—which was revealed in the Son of God, when he took little children in his arms, and blessed them; when He stood at the grave of Lazarus, and wept there. The showers that fall in their shining beauty out of the skies—dropping upon the earth in its spring-tide, and giving brightness to the blossom, and fruitful life to all the scene—they come as blessings descending upon the earth, and we may well be grateful for them. But they are not tears of personal sympathy, falling upon us from the eyes of Omnipotence. They are the fluent crystal jewels, scattered from the casket which is full of such treasures. But when I see the Lord himself, who has all might and government in his hand, standing before the grave of his friend, and weeping there—it is more to me than all spring showers! For there is the spirit, not of wisdom alone, or of bounteous compassion, but of tenderest sympathy, behind the tears; and my heart swells and melts as I read of it.

So nowhere in the material universe do we see declared, in its most complete and impressive exhibition, that infinite love which was in Christ toward the world of mankind; that love which led him even to the cross, and the sacrifice of himself, for our advantage. All other manifestations, therefore, of that which is really Divine in character, are pale and poor by the side of this. You tell me of the Southern Cross, lifting its stars in the sky that bends beyond the horizon;

and that shall be to me a symbol perhaps, almost a foreshadowing, but it never is the parallel, of this cross upon Calvary. This shines with no starry splendor upon the earth. Over it was gathered, rather, the shrouding of a supernatural darkness, from the sixth hour to the ninth. But the lesson that comes from it is the grandest and most precious the world has heard. The cross lifted among the stars, in those yet unseen Southern skies, tells of the power of him who built it. But the cross so stained, and dark, and bloody, that was lifted on Calvary, tells of the infinite and unsearchable love in the heart of him who hung upon it. From this we get views, therefore, which we cannot from any part of the universe that sweeps its radiant circles above us—which we cannot from even the soul of man, to which this outward is the setting—of the character of God; not of his infinite righteousness, only, but of his eternal and measureless love; of his sympathy with the suffering; of his incomparable and unconquerable patience, toward even those who sin against him.

And it is not till a character harmonious with this has been developed and cultivated within us—till we have throned in our own souls the righteousness and the love, the sympathy and the patience, which are infinite in God—it is not till *then* that the welfare of the soul, living and personal, and made in his image, has been secured. Christ alone fully reveals to us this character. He alone helps us, by his truth, his example, and the gift of his Spirit, to reproduce it in ourselves. And he who wins a soul to Him has thus again aided to secure for it the essential well-being which it needs, and which, when gained, shall be as immortal as itself!

But we need of course to add another, a third element—as also implied in the consummate and enduring welfare of the soul—THE DEVELOPMENT WITHIN IT OF ITS GOD-LIKE POWERS: the development of these powers in such a way, and to such a degree, that it shall be fitted for the largest operation, the grandest offices, that can be ever opened to it. This must also be gained through Christ. And he who leads a soul to Him, does for it in *this* regard what no other could.

There is a reserve of power in the soul, that never appears till the time of some great crisis has come; that possibly never appears at all, on this side of eternity. Did you ever seriously think of the fact that the power of enjoying the beauty of a statue, the power of appreciating the glory of architecture in some immense and majestic cathedral, the power of feeling, enjoying, appreciating, the witchery of some charming poem, the lyric or the epic—that this familiar and customary power, of which so often we are conscious, may be really a power, when the germ that lies in it has been developed, of creating that which now it admires? Its tendency is to arise to that. So there are hidden moral forces, as well as mental, that do not come out until some great emergency in experience awakens and shows them. How often do we see, thus, the timid, retiring, and sensitive woman, who has been accustomed wholly to depend upon companions and friends for support, in the front of some terrific disaster, when Death stands imminent, remaining serene, and utterly self-poised, while all around are shrinking in affright; or, in the hour of unexpected and appalling adversity, standing, not stunned but keenly sensitive, and fully alive to the facts she has to meet, yet not excited on the other hand, but calm and tranquil in the midst of the adversity—showing a central might in her spirit, which we should never have imagined to belong to it; which was not realized even to her consciousness, and would not have been, except for such a tremendous experience.

Now when you look at these forces in their germ, who shall say to what height of development they may not amid immortality arise? Quickened even here by the truth, the grace, and the spirit of Christ, and hereafter set free from their present limitations, in the realms which he has prepared for his people, there seems no term conceivable by us which they may not arrive at and surpass. You take the grandest human soul that you have known, or have read of in history —the most masterly mind, or the most supreme and electrifying will, that has come within the circle of your observation, or that has shed its lustre heretofore on the annals of the race,—and that after all but gives you a hint of what you may yourself become, and shall assuredly by-and-by become, if your powers are unfolded and cultured as they may be, as they must be to the consummate well-being of the soul. As the Apostle John saith: "It doth not yet appear what we shall be." You take the poet, in that hour of ecstasy, when his imagination glows and is exalted, and when his tongue is touched and loosened with a strange inspiration—when words come twin-born with the thoughts that are luminous and high, and the syllables which to you are difficult flow chiming in music from his entranced transfigured lips—and even that marvel of mental experience doth not show us fully what we may become! At some time or other, if Christ hath done his work in us, the state we reach may so far transcend this, that it shall have been but a distant prophecy of what we know in realization. And no other mental or moral attainment ever yet accomplished on earth can show us, more than by partial hints, what we ourselves may through the Son and the Spirit of God aspire to reach.

We must gain this, then,—this amplest development which is possible for us,—in order to our complete well-being. No matter what treasures of wealth we have, nor what pleasures we enjoy, I submit to you all that the immortal welfare of the soul, supreme and consummate, will never have been realized till these things are accomplished in it, and accomplished for it; till it is reconciled with its Maker, through faith in Christ, and repentance from sin; till in it has been developed and cultivated a God-like character, such as was revealed, present and personal, through the incarnation of Christ, and through his subsequent work and suffering; till there have been unfolded in it those grandest faculties, not as yet fully revealed, in which the condition and the basis are shown of a glory that we cannot yet comprehend; till we have thus become prepared for the largest operation, the grandest offices, which even immortality shall open to us! All this is implied in God's amazing constitution of our being. And he who wins a soul to Christ, sets it forth on its progress toward this attainment; a progress to which no reach of our thought can fix a limit.

And fourthly, and finally, as the fruit of all these, comes the last element now to be specified as essential to the perfect well-being of the soul: A CONSTANT, SWEET, AND IMMORTAL FELICITY, in the presence of God, in sympathy with him, and with the Seraphim and the Saints who are gathered about him; a felicity that shall flow like a river in the soul, deep and bright, filling it with its rich experience; a felicity that shall be as a shining atmosphere around that soul—beneath whose radiance all spiritual graces shall start forth and flourish; in whose inspiration, each voice shall be one of constant song, and every thought of joy and praise!

We do not feel that we have realized a true or a sufficient welfare, even in this world, until we are in the conscious experience of that inmost happiness which comes from virtue. We never can attain our consummate welfare in the world to come—all that of which we are capable by nature, and toward which the soul constitutionally aspires—till this virtue has been perfected, and this happiness made supreme. But when our relations with God are harmonious, when in us has been completely developed that Divine character which was revealed in Christ our Lord, when our powers are unfolded, and prepared for every grandest service to which they can be called, then joy must become our continual experience. Then shall the perfect blessedness which we feel, and which we see revealed on all sides, be as the walls of precious stones, circling around us; and as the pavements of transparent gold, beneath our feet; as the rainbow, arching in its prismatic beauty before our eyes; as the river of the water of life which we drink of, and the tree of life, of whose shade and fruit we constantly partake.

The soul will then have at last attained its true well-being, to which no element need be added. And that well-being shall be as eternal as is the being of God Himself! The stars that we look at in yonder skies shall fade from the sight of men and of angels. It is only a difference of time, after all, between the glittering coruscation of the meteors, which flash into our atmosphere and die there, and the shining of the orbs which seem to be set eternally in their places. These still are transient, like the meteors. The difference between them is a difference of years. The sun himself shall be extinguished, as are the flames which now his brighter light puts out; and the star that looks most steadfast in the heavens is moving constantly toward its dissolution. But the soul which scans, measures, and weighs these, outlasts them all. An effect wrought on it becomes immortal. And so the effort that seeks its good vindicates itself as the wisest of Time.

You build your house; and the changes of enterprise may sweep it from the earth. It must by-and-by return to dust. You gather your fortune; and time, and change, and death, shall scatter it, to every wind. You frame your policy of government and statesmanship; and the coming years shall overwhelm it in forgetfulness. You utter, in volumes ornate and eloquent, your theories of Science and of Art; and shortly men forget the fact that they were ever wrought out and published. You win a human soul to Christ, and you have enriched the universe forever!

It is only when we look at this, from this point of view, that we understand the construction of the BIBLE, so wonderful as it is, involving so many diverse minds, extending over so many centuries, but bearing all and always, consistently, upon one point: the winning of souls of men to Christ!

It is only when we look at this, too, from this point of view, that we understand the reason of MIRACLES, or can appreciate the argument for them. Men say, 'It is incredible that God should work miracles, interrupting thus the order of his universe, and breaking in abruptly upon its harmonies.' But the most stupendous miracle of the Scriptures is plainly just as possible to God as is breath or pulsation to you and me. It is his will, alone, that forbids them, in the usual order of the creation. It is his will that equally accomplishes them, when the exigency which calls for them has come. And there is nothing incredible about them, when we remember the purpose which they serve: that they are wrought for bringing back the Race which has fallen, into its just relations to himself. The moment we look from this point upon them, we understand the reason of Miracles, and even feel them probable beforehand. What could not be accomplished by human instrumentality, nor through the usual operations of nature, that God in his mercy seeks to accomplish through wonders and visions, through convulsions of the earth, and sudden terrors of tempest in the air. And these are just as reasonable and credible as are the silent operations of his Spirit in the hearts of men.

It is only under the light of the same theme that we understand the work and sacrifice of Christ himself: the most wonderful of all miracles, the most transcendent of all the Divine operations in the world, his INCARNATION, and his DEATH. Not to found a new empire, however magnificent, not to create a new planet or sun, would the Son of God have become incarnate, in the feeble babe of the manger at Bethlehem.

There was no necessity, to such an effect, for such a superlative condescension. He might speak, and it should be done. The mere mandate unuttered, existing in his mind, would strew this moment the silent heavens with other worlds, and fill those spaces of void darkness which the astronomer finds between the stars, with clusters of universes grander still than that to which our earth belongs. There was no possible need of his Death, to accomplish such a work as this. There is no work whatever, save one, yet known to us, that can interpret and justify the sacrifice, so immense, and so transcendent. And this one work is that of "winning souls" to God, and making their immortality glorious, through their restored relations to him. When we think of this, the Incarnation is harmonized with the whole Divine plan; and even the sacrifice of Calvary itself is justified to our minds!

And this alone interprets, as well, the mission and work of the HOLY SPIRIT; that constant miracle of the Christian dispensation, which we have witnessed in the midst of us, which many of us have felt, I trust, in our own hearts; that miracle by which the Divine power that brought the order out of the chaos, that wrought on the troubled elements of the earth, and made it a solid and fruitful orb for us to inhabit, comes to-day as a still small voice, yet works in men with the mystery of Omnipotence! It comes, not as the glory came upon Sinai, making the crags to reel and quake, the mountain rock. It comes into our souls more gently than the breath of your babe breathes against your cheek, in its calm sleep! It comes into our souls more sweetly than does the delicate strain of music, which the ear must listen intently to catch; more gently than does even the voice of a friend, bringing some message of peace to our hearts. And only by the train of thought we have followed are we prepared for that wondrous operation by which this eternal Spirit of God enters so silently, yet so effectually, into the soul, to make it God-like, first in character, then in power, and to fill it with the experience of His favor.

"He that winneth souls is wise." And God himself never reveals his wisdom more distinctly to us, and to the angels overhead, than when he works his miracles for this end; when he sends his Son into the world to die, for the same end; when he sends his Spirit into the estranged hearts of men, that he may bring them back to himself. He illustrates his wisdom more vividly here, than when he made the universe march in shining order before his throne, and set its worlds worlds in the orbits they maintain!

In the light of this, we see, my Brethren, the glory

of the CHURCH, as an institution for the winning of souls to God and Christ; how it is that it continues from age to age, with a glory that does not pass away, and that pertains to no other institution. The purpose which it serves marks it divine. If it were to seek any secular end—to attempt, as in time past the acquisition of wealth, or the subjugation of empires to itself,—it would come under the law of other similar institutions, becoming transient in its continuance, and imperfect in its claim on men's allegiance. But so long as the purpose to which it steadfastly adheres is the conversion of mankind unto God, it abides, and must prosper. Its glory is inherent. You cannot add to it by any accumulation of visible powers, or by clothing with any titles its ministers. 'By the Church,' said the Apostle,—and remember that he was writing to the poor converts of the earliest century, very imperfect in their character, very limited in their influence, who were gathered at Ephesus, and the various near commercial cities,—'by the Church,' made up of the ignorant and the weak, of slaves and of the outcast—'by the Church may be made known,'—made known to whom? to the world around it? Nay, verily!—'by the Church may be made known to Principalities and Powers in heavenly places, the manifold wisdom of God!'

For "he that winneth souls is wise." And however humble the Church may be, by its agency in bringing men to Christ—through its ministry of the truth, when that is accompanied by the grace of the Highest—the manifold wisdom of the Creator is revealed, even to angels in heavenly places; is so revealed as it could not be in all wonders of Creation, and all the mighty order of Providence.

At the same point we learn to appreciate also the glory and privilege of the work of the MINISTER, in the Church. The glory, and the privilege, of it! Remember how Paul felt concerning this, as it is illustrated in the passage from his first epistle to the Corinthians which I have read in your hearing this morning. "Necessity is laid upon me," he says, "to preach the Gospel." 'It is not a necessity of occupation, or of support! I might be an officer in the Jewish Church, I might be an officer in the Roman State.' To a man of Paul's capacity and culture—his energy of mind, and his power of will—all offices were open; every avenue that led to prominence and power. He was himself a Roman citizen, as well as of the choicest Hebrew stock. But "necessity is laid upon me," he says. 'Because of the love I bear to the Master, who brought the Gospel of peace to the world, and who for it laid down his life,—because of the greatness, intrinsic and unspeakable, of the work to be performed,—I *must* preach the word. To them that are under the law, I become as under the law myself, that I may bring them to the liberty of the Gospel. To those without law, I become as without law, that I may bring them under the rule of love and of Christ. I am made all things to all men, that I may by all means save some.' For this is a work whose rewards are intrinsic, and whose effects are eternal; and "he that winneth souls is wise."

This has seemed to me, my Brethren, a theme especially appropriate to us to-day. I finish, with the day, the last sabbath of Twenty successive years of my Ministry, in this parish and Church. It is an occasion on which I naturally look backward, as you also look backward—many of you over several years, some of you to the very beginning, of this ministry. And standing here to-day I rejoice anew in this Church of Christ; in the work which has been accomplished by it; in the influence which has gone out from it; in the harmony and prosperity which God has given to it from the outset; most of all in the souls which have been, in it, and by it, brought back to God.

When I came into the pastorate here, there had been one hundred and forty-two persons received into the Church; two of them upon confession of faith, one hundred and forty upon letters of dismission from other Churches. Of that whole number there are about thirty remaining still on the roll of our members. But five or six of these are absent from the Church, living in distant parts of the city, or in other cities, and only occasionally uniting with us, and partaking of our communion. So that there are but about twenty-five of those who were members of the Church when I came here, who are still present and active in it.

Since the commencement of my ministry, there have been received into the Church, on confession of their faith, three hundred and ninety-four persons—or nearly twenty for every year; and, on letters from other Churches, six hundred and seventeen; making a total of one thousand and eleven.

From the beginning of the history of the Church, extending over nearly two years before I came to it as its pastor, there have been received three hundred and ninety-six upon confession, and seven hundred and fifty-seven upon letters; making a total number of one thousand one hundred and fifty-three. Of these, ninty-four have died; and four hundred and eighty-three have been removed, by dismission or otherwise; making five hundred and seventy-seven who have left the Church, after being at some time connected with it; while five hundred and seventy-six remain,—or, as nearly as possible, one half of the number. One year's record will illustrate the extent and the rapidity of the changes we have seen. There were received into the Church during the first year of my ministry to it, sixty-nine persons; twelve upon confession of faith, and fifty-seven upon Church letters. Of these, fourteen have died; thirty-four have been dismissed;

and six are only occasionally with us; leaving but fifteen still at home in the Church, of all who in that year of our history became identified with us.

During the present year, sixty-eight have been received to the Church, on confession of their faith, and thirty-four upon letters from abroad; making one hundred and two in all, or the largest number ever yet received in a single year to our communion. In the city, at the time when I came to it, there was but one other Church of the same order with this, and that a small one, encumbered with debt, which a few years afterward was wholly merged in another organization. Now in this city, and its vicinity on the Island, there are eighteen Churches of our faith and order; all of them prosperous, nearly all of them self-sustaining, and some of them among the strongest in the land.

In reckoning rapidly the sums which have been contributed here, during these years, to the various objects of Christian benevolence,—and including some which have not passed through the general treasury of the Church, but have been given by individuals for particular institutions or purposes of beneficence, outside our usual contributions,—I find that $220,000 have been given for objects wholly apart from our own expenses. More, rather than less, than this sum, has certainly been thus contributed, for religious, philanthropic, and educational uses. And the harvest of influences, of which the seed has in this way been sown, the coming centuries will continue to garner.

This is a very imperfect summary of what has been done here. But even this—how large is the work which it represents! Some of you have been associated for enterprises that are great and signal in the eyes of men. Standing in this pulpit to-day, and looking back over these Twenty years of our Church history, I feel that you ought most of all to rejoice that you have been permitted to take part in this, which is the grandest of all that have invited you: an enterprise for the glory of God, in the immortal salvation of men. He who sends the lightning under the sea, and makes it carry human thought through the abysmal darkness there, is wise, no doubt; and he who stretches the lines of railway over the continent; and he who builds the great institutions of society and of government. But one man is wiser than either, or than all: he who gives of his substance, of his time and enthusiasm, and his personal endeavor, to the establishment or to the enlargement of that Church of Christ whose office it is to win souls to God.

For myself I rejoice, as I look back over these rapid years, in the work it has been permitted to me to assist, or to do. I rejoice to acknowledge the uniform kindness which has from the first been manifested toward me in this congregation, and the help which I have always derived from your sympathies and prayers, and your intelligent coöperating exertions. I rejoice to feel that these years are secure! that nothing whatever, which may occur in the Future, can change, or mar, or blot them out!

There may have been fifty persons, I suppose—I know of certainly more than thirty—who have been hopefully led to Christ in this congregation, coming under my personal ministry, as well as under the general ministry of the truth from this pulpit, who yet have not connected themselves with this Church. They were tarrying here only for the time, and returned to different parts of the country after their conversion, forming connection with Churches there, where their residence was to be. And out of this entire number, of four hundred and thirty, or four hundred and fifty, thus led to Christ, I have scarcely known a single one who has given occasion to doubt the reality of the change which appeared, or the realness and power of the Christian experience.—No man can rob me of the joy of having been the instrument under God of leading these souls, so far as I have helped to lead them, unto the knowledge and love of Christ! For all the wealth of the cities of the world, I would not exchange that blessed recollection! Thank God for the privilege of the work of the Ministry! Thank God for the grace which put me into it!

To-day, my Brethren, we are again called to give—as we have been many times before called to give—to the maintenance and enlargement of the "City Mission and Tract Society;" with which this Church has been closely associated from the beginning of its history; to which it is but justice to say that it has contributed certainly as much, not of money alone, but of moral influence, and of energy and skill in the direction of its affairs, as any other in the city. I remember the first year on which we took our public collection for this Society—which was then confined chiefly to the work of distributing tracts in the city. We took up, by a great exertion, a collection amounting to not more than four hundred dollars; my impression is that it was a little less than that sum. The last year, our collection for the same object, was four thousand five hundred dollars. And this was secured with far less effort upon my part than had been needful for the other.

The Society had, twenty years ago, but a single missionary in the field. It now has Twenty. We have gained one for every year since I first pleaded in this pulpit in its behalf. I have been unsuccessful in my effort to obtain the number of conversions reported by our diligent missionaries, in the course of these years. But they have been certainly many hundreds, I think some thousands. God has constantly blessed the efforts which they have made, with the accompanying grace of his Spirit. And the number of those who have, either directly or indirectly, been reached and moved, and led to Christ, through their labors, only Omniscience can record.

To-day, then,—standing at the end of these years

and looking back together upon them with gratitude to God, and praises for his goodness to us,—let us make, through this beloved Society, a thank-offering to Him for the kindness which has spared us to each other so long, and give more largely than ever before for its good work:—a work to be accomplished in the city around us, to which we shall look back with delight when the Future has opened to us its vision and reward! It can hardly be possible, in the nature of things, that more than a majority of us should be gathered again at the end of another Twenty years of the ministry of the Gospel in this place; hardly in the nature of things be possible that to me it should be given to minister to you in the future so long. But whensoever the time of separation shall come, whensoever the voice that calls us hence shall make itself heard, saying to each of us, 'Come up higher, and I will show thee things that shall be hereafter,'—God grant that we may be able to look back upon this work as nobly done : so nobly and so generously done that it shall have lent a new inspiration to other churches to do their share of the same work more vigorously than ever; so generously done that by it the reign of the Lord and of his Gospel shall be grandly extended throughout this city, in which God has given to us our dwelling.

My dear Friends, who are still not united to Christ, I cannot close without one word on this anniversary to you to whom I have preached so often, and who have yet failed to respond to my words; who have not found, and have not sought, that reconciliation with God through Christ, to which I have tried so earnestly to lead you, and without which the whole world given to you would only leave you poorer than before! "He that winneth souls is wise." Would that I were wise enough to know by what argument which I never have mastered, by what appeal which I have never been able to make, I could now reach and stir your hearts! If he that winneth souls is wise, oh! do not forget—I pray you to-day, do *not* forget—that he who giveth his soul to God is wise forever; and he who refuses to do that—notwithstanding all God's goodness to him, and all the lessons that come from experience, and all the appeals that flow from the Cross, and all the solemn adjurations of Eternity—he is, in the deepest and most absolute sense, unwise for himself—unwise forever!

EVENING SERMON.

1st Thessalonians, 3 : 8.

"FOR NOW WE LIVE, IF YE STAND FAST IN THE LORD."

It seems at first sight an extraordinary thing that these words should have been written by him who sent them, to those to whom they were addressed. Paul does not seem to us a man especially dependent on the sympathy of others, for his enjoyment, or for his vigor of purpose and of will. Until we have penetrated beneath the primary aspects of his character, and have touched his inmost heart and spirit, until we have found what a deep and delicate sensibility was in him, how eager and tender were his affections, we do not suspect his dependence on others, or appreciate the intimate consciousness which he shows of the inspiriting influence of his friend's enthusiasm. What, therefore, would have seemed but natural in John, that sensitive, responsive, almost feminine disciple, who was manifestly moved by the moods of others, and inflamed by their ardor, and whose ultimate self-reliance had required many years and large discipline to complete it,—this does not at once impress us, I think, as what was to be expected in the resolute, fearless, and firm-nerved Paul, who was not afraid of an empire in arms, who bore on himself the concentrated care of all the churches, and whose serene and self-poised fortitude rose to only fresh mastery as the difficulty and danger gathered thicker about him. We are hardly prepared to hear *him* say, 'Now does our spiritual life, for its fulness and blessedness, depend upon yours!' But we look, rather, to find him always the source and spring of inspiration to others; the steadfast and imperial teacher, who imparts to them knowledge, and from contact with whose illuminated mind their convictions are constantly renewed; the self-sufficing heroic champion, by whom they are guided, encouraged, defended, but to whom they—because of their immense inferiority, because of his so singular completeness—can render nothing in return.

We need to know the Apostle more fully, to have walked with him familiarly throughout his epistles, to have marked the kindness and the generous gentleness in which he abounded, to have seen how lonely he felt himself in solitude, how his very heart ached for society and sympathy at Athens and at Rome, and how he was refreshed by these the moment they met him,—we need to have seen how capacious that princely nature was of all tenderest emotion, while also so stocked with the manliest strength,—before we can clearly understand how it was that he should say, 'Now is our state of force and of felicity conditioned upon yours. If ye stand fast in the Lord, we live.'

Nor is it less remarkable, at first sight, that he should have said this to those to whom he did say it; to those who had been converted to Christ in Thessalonica. They were not many. They were by no means eminent, strong, or cultivated Christians. They had lately been brought to the knowledge of the Lord by Paul himself, who had preached to them a few weeks on his way along the seaboard, from Philippi to Athens. They dwelt in a city, not distinguished above others perhaps for the corruptness of its manners, but which—like all the great commercial towns of that most frivolous and licentious age—was pervaded by heathenism, and full of vice; and which lately had taken a bad preëminence through the violence of the assault permitted in it on the Apostle himself, and on those who believed with him. Fewer of the Hebrews had here been converted than was common elsewhere, and a larger proportion than usual of the church was made up of those who had just turned from the worship of idols. Among them, too, an incipient heresy had already begun to manifest and to spread itself, concerning the time of the Lord's second coming, and concerning the state of those who should die before that event. Some, in their restless expectation of the Lord, were disposed to be idle, and careless of their customary duties in the world; others to be turbulent and refractory in the Church, and, under pretence of edifying each other, to spread disorder in their infant community. And, on the whole, looking back to it from our times, it would hardly seem that any Church thus far established would be less likely than this of the Thessalonians to render to Paul any spiritual help.

That he should therefore express to them—whom he had not known long, whom he himself had just led forth from the darkness and grossness of Pagan idolatries, who seemed to be utterly dependent upon him, and upon the messages and the letters he should send them, for spiritual strength, wisdom and culture,— that he should express so emphatically to *them* his sense of the support and the quickening encouragement to be derived by himself from their fidelity,— even more than this: his sense of his need of just such support, as the vital condition of his own completest spiritual life,—this may well seem extraordinary! It may look, almost, like a phrase of mere courtesy; a graceful and conciliatory address of compliment, which shows that he remembered and kindly regarded them, but which is not to be taken in its exact and literal force. We may even be tempted, perhaps, to suspect that he flatters them a little, in this delicate way, in order to commend to them more effectually the precepts and instructions with which the Epistle is elsewhere replete.

And yet, if we thoughtfully consider it, my Friends, we shall see that this is not so; that these, above others, were the disciples who might most fitly encourage and inspire the veteran Apostle. Because they had recently been converted to Christ—many of them from the midst of heathenism—Paul longed the more earnestly to hear of their fidelity, and would take a fresh stimulation and strength from the tidings thereof. Because they were surrounded with temptation and peril, their steadfastness in their allegiance to Christ would re-enforce and invigorate him, for the work which was to come, more than could almost anything beside. And if, with the evident tendencies to error in doctrine, and to errors of practice, which already surrounded and were subtly affecting them, they still remained true to the Master and his Gospel, then would Paul preach in every community which he thenceforth should enter, with a more settled and central confidence, the principles and the promises which had proved in their experience so mighty and benign.

It was not, therefore, a matter of compliment—it was not a formal expression of courtesy—this which the now mature Apostle, who had been for many years a disciple, and for most of them a preacher of the word, sent to those recent, few, and poor Thessalonian converts, when he said, "For now we live, if ye stand fast in the Lord." The vital bond which always connects the Teacher with the taught, and makes them reciprocally helpful to each other—the disciples often as useful to the Teacher, in advancing and finishing his force and his culture, as he can have been at the outset to them,—this is here recognized, with only the greater distinctness and emphasis by reason of the character and the peculiar relation of him who speaks, and of those to whom his words are addressed. And for this important general truth, which is involved in the text, we may profitably pause this evening to ponder it.

If Paul could say it to those with whom he had tarried so briefly, and who were necessarily known to him so slightly—if he could say it, who seemed to need, almost to admit, no help or addition from any quarter, to complete him in his culture, or confirm him in his strength—how much more may any Pastor now say it, who dwells with one people year after year; who comes into constant intercourse with them; and who occupies a far lower position toward them, as a Christian instructor, than that which Paul held toward those recent converts to whom he wrote; who is conscious, too, of weaknesses and wants from which the great Apostle to the Gentiles was conspicuously exempt! How much more earnestly and emphatically may *he* say—with what almost vehemence may he repeat the declaration—'Now do I live,' in the best Christian attainment and enjoyment, in the richest experience of knowledge, love, and spiritual power, in the most effective Christian usefulness, if, and only if, ye who hear me 'stand fast in the Lord!'

The beneficial spiritual influence which the members of a Church naturally exert upon their Pastor may be distributed under these main divisions :

First. Their influence on his knowledge and belief of the Christian system, as they confirm and renew these; as they make them practical, and not simply theoretic—matters of experience, fruits of observation, and not mere conclusions drawn from argument and from study.

Second. Their influence on his zeal in his work, as they quicken and increase this, and sometimes inflame it—through the example and contact of their own—to an ardent enthusiasm.

Third. Their direct influence on his character, as they impart to this, silently, gradually, of the beauty, richness, and virtue of their own ; as they complete it, from their more various and affluent excellence, or reduce what in it is abnormal and excessive, by the suggestions, or the positive attrition, of their better symmetry. And,

Fourth. Their influence on his sense of effective and large usefulness in his work ; as they distribute his influence more widely than he could possibly have personally carried it; as through their lips, and lives, and charities, the forces which he has set in operation are made to sweep a far broader circumference than his most intense and unremitting activity could ever have covered.

It is not necessary that I develope in detail each or either of these several points. A glance at them, in their series, or separately, will suffice to show that the general principle, inferred from the special words of the Apostle, is forevermore true; that reciprocity of communication must always exist between the preacher and the people; and that while he is acting upon them for their good, they also in turn react upon him, and injure or benefit him, with an efficiency greater, to a degree more important, than they themselves are always aware of. Their height and reach of Christian attainment are in fact the conditions, as well as the exponents, of his own. And not more depends, for the growth, welfare, and usefulness of a Church, on what he brings them, than on how they receive it, and what is the tribute they render for it, in the influence which they reflect upon himself.

As human nature is constituted and trained, this cannot be otherwise. We are necessarily dependent, each upon the other; and none is so wholly complete on all sides that he does not require, as none is so hard that he does not feel, what is brought him by others. The force which is contained, too, in a whole congregation—in which the many minds and wills are substantially harmonized—is of course more solid, more abounding and comprehensive, and more impressive, than that which can emanate from any one person. It is a life-force, not a mere intellectual influence; and though it acts silently, it acts continuously, with a certain direct dynamic energy. He who is embosomed in it may not feel so much his special indebtedness to particular individuals, as they may feel their indebtedness to him. But he will and must feel, he cannot escape feeling, his dependence on the whole, and the aids to growth, the impulse to enterprise, or the contrary influences toward coldness and indolence, which they impart.

Let a Minister stand year after year in a sluggish, unintelligent, unresponsive congregation, whose members receive his weekly lessons, but make for them no positive and animating spiritual returns—who are listless and worldly in their prevalent temper, and who have not learned the blessing and the joy of active exertion in the cause of the Master; let him be met with a passive indifference when he opens to them the truth, and especially when he seeks to unfold that truth in its more delicate harmonies, or its remoter relations; let it all be accepted as a creditable enough performance on his part, which he was to exhibit, while the people sat to pass judgment upon it, and the ultimate fruit of which is to be their transient mental entertainment; let him be encircled, when he speaks to them in familiar converse, not with a sweet and sunny spirit of Christian sympathy, charity, hope, or a radiant outgush of Christian affection,—but, with a shrewd worldly sagacity, with a frivolous temper that treats all the facts of the Gospel as unreal, and its maxims as unpractical, or with a sharp and hard-edged censoriousness that cuts the life out from all Christian development; and let him feel that what he says produces no beneficial impression outside the circle which he himself immediately addresses,—that no helpful hands are carrying it further, and no earnest voices are dispensing it to the poor, and no rich charities are conveying it round the world;—let this be his attitude, and this his environment, and you might as well put the man at the poles, in the heart of an ice-berg, walled up all around with gelid pinnacles, and expect him to maintain his vital warmth in that austere and clasping cold, as put him in such a pulpit as that, and expect him to continue a faithful, earnest, and quickening preacher.

His manner will freeze, if his spirit does not; and deeper and deeper the chill will strike, as he tarries there longer, till he comes to be as impassive as his people. He must enkindle a light in their souls, or find the light in his put out. If he cannot melt their flinty frost, and touch with fire their dull sensibilities, through the fervor of his faith, they will at last chill him to the centre. 'Now I might have lived,' such a man may say at the end of his ministry, 'if ye had only been faithful and earnest! But the steady pull of your continuous and unsubduable worldliness has carried me with it in its downward drift. Ye have quenched what ardor of soul I had; and have made my ministry degenerate at last into a matter of mere routine, or have even perverted it into heresy. And the shame and the crime of this consummation are not mine alone; they belong to us both!' How many there have been who have had such a ministry, and who might have given this witness at its close!

But, on the other hand, suppose a man brought year after year into contact with minds that are active, responsive, and full of inquiries concerning the truth, —not skeptically questioning, but candidly and variously considering that truth, and seeking to gain of it the largest knowledge; suppose him to see the effect of his ministry in souls convinced, persuaded, converted, and filled with new-born joy and song;—suppose him, as he visits from house to house, to be commonly accosted by Christian faith, patience, and peace, even where trouble and anxiety are found, much more in the homes of comfort and prosperity; to be encircled, in the assemblies of his people, by an earnest desire for the furtherance of the Gospel, and a hearty enthusiasm—that prompts to personal effort and sacrifice—for the conversion of men to Christ; suppose him to meet resignation and hope, or the more vivid triumphs of faith, at the death-bed and the grave; a holy gratitude in the house filled with joy by the bridal or the birth; an unflinching fidelity to the principles of righteousuess, in the day of sore commercial trial; a tranquil trustfulness, and a happy submission, at the bedside where month after month has passed, and left the suffering form still prostrate, with no rescue by medicine, and no prospect but of death;—and suppose him to know, beyond all this, that far outside the limits of his parish, those forming it are going on errands of mercy and good-will to others, are scattering whatever of light he brings them throughout the chambers of ignorance and of sin, are carrying it abroad, by systematic and large contributions, to distant frontiers, and over the breadth of foreign lands;—suppose *this* to be his position and his experience, and he may say with utmost emphasis, not, 'Now live I, IF ye stand fast in the Lord!' but, 'Now live I, in the noblest power and peace of the soul, BECAUSE ye have stood fast in the faith, and in the Master from whom we both have received and have learned it! Your staunch fidelity has been my shield and my support! Your zeal, the spring from which my earnestness has been always replenished! Your submission and hope, my constant inspiration! And much as I may have given to you, in public ministry, or in private communion, that, and much more, have ye returned, in these your silent reciprocal ministrations!'

So, plainly, may any Minister affirm, whose fortunate lot has placed him with a people susceptible to the influences which he brings them from the Gospel, and accustomed to reproduce those influences in their conduct and character. That conduct, and that character, must inevitably become more to him than all treatises of religion, and all lessons of the schools. His own convictions of the truth must be vitalized, through the effects it works among his people. A constant influence raining on him, from their uplifted and consecrated souls, must enlighten and invigorate him; while, with a sense of ample efficiency to which others are strangers, may he, amid whatever of weakness, accomplish through them his work for the Master.

One of the greatest and sorest trials,—though one at the same time less generally appreciated than are some minor physical inconveniences—which front the missionary in foreign lands, or in our own recent and untamed territories, is this of having to work alone; of wanting that encouragement which can come only from a surrounding and inspiriting sympathy; of feeling the chill of an atmosphere full on every side of skeptical scoffing and of ribald confusion; of thinking, as did the prophet of old, that he alone, of all the multitude, is not now bowing the knee to Baal. And one of the great and stimulating advantages which invest the ministry, as exercised in communities long subject to the Gospel, and pervaded by its force,—and especially as exercised in Churches where the pastor and the people dwell permanently together, in a cordial alliance—is this of deriving both inward comfort and outward help from the faith of great numbers;

of staying the spirit when it otherwise would have sunk, overborne by fatigues or desponding through discouragements, on the prayers, the convictions, the expectations, and the labors, which are ever anew supplied by others. A blessed thing it is, indeed, for any Minister to be able to say to the people over whom he watches in the Gospel; 'Now do I live because ye all stand fast in the Lord!' Your vigor invigorates, your enthusiasm refreshes, your temper refines, exalts, completes, your knowledge enlarges and clarifies mine! And while I may give to individuals among you more spiritual help than they in turn can render to me, the body of Christ, which you compose, is my most efficient instructor, under God. Through it, as through a palpable medium, the grace of the Highest flows in upon my soul. By my continual contacts with it are kept full the springs of my spiritual power and life!

In some good measure, at least, my Brethren, I can say this of this beloved Church; and therefore this theme has seemed very naturally to suggest itself this evening. Once before I have preached on it—years ago—in this same pulpit; rather as suggesting at that time, however, a theme of exhortation, which it seemed my duty to bring to you. To-night I preach upon it again, at this last service of Twenty years of my Ministry in this parish, as suggesting a theme of grateful acknowledgment which it is my privilege to present.

I should not be true to my own consciousness of the help which you have continually given me, if I did not present it, as I review, from this latest hour, the time which has so swiftly passed.

I do not certainly intend to affirm—you would not believe me if I did, and would not credit me with sincerity in saying it,—that this has been a perfect Church. As we measure it against the ideal of the New Testament, which will in future times be realized, it has been far enough from that; and none can feel its deficiencies more keenly than those who have long been associated with it, and accustomed to pray for its perfection. But without the smallest disposition to exaggerate, or, certainly, to flatter—which you will bear witness that I have not been wont to do hitherto, and which I do not intend at this late day to begin,—I may say, as a reason for grateful acknowledgment to God for his goodness, that nowhere in the land, in all the wide circle of Churches of different names to which I have occasionally ministered, have I found another more full than this of intellectual and spiritual force; more attentive to the truth, or more responsive to its appeals; more ready to give, and personally to labor, for the advancement of the kingdom of Christ; more eager and tender in its solicitous sympathies toward those who are inquiring for the way and the hope of the life everlasting; more glad and grateful, when God has been pleased to bless it in his grace—as from time to time he has done—with signal and powerful effusions of his Spirit; more ready to seize on every opportunity to make an influence for goodness and for God widely felt in the land and the world.

I never preach to another congregation which I so well love to address as my own. I have never known, since my ministry began here, another Church that seemed to me,—in all the influence which pervaded it, —more helpful and useful than this has been to those embraced in its communion. And it is delightful to me to know, as it must be equally so to you, that those who have gone forth from us in the past, and who are now scattered in distant places or other lands, still feel toward this Church as we do who have tarried in it; and that their hearts untraveled return, in frequent thought and affectionate remembrance, to the services in which they here have united, and the solemn or the joyful scenes which they have witnessed beneath this roof.

Looking back then over the past to-night, I recognize, and joyfully express and record, my sense of personal spiritual indebtedness to you my people. I know full well that to many among you it has pleased our Father to make me at times of special service: in helping to sustain you, in the hour of sore bereavement and sorrow; in helping to enlighten you, when questions concerning the truth or your duty were pressing darkly upon your minds; in helping to lead you to new efforts of Christian endurance and enterprise, or new victories of faith, when you were tempted to faint and despond; in helping to guide you into the way of pardon and peace, when your steps had been arrested by the precepts of Christ, when your souls were stirred with the sense of immortality, and when the path which you eagerly sought seemed hard to gain. As I said in the morning, the richest reward of my work here—next to the hope of the approval of the Master—is the consciousness I rejoice in of having been an instrument of blessing and help to many among you.

But you have also helped me in return; and have ministered to me, not of material things alone, but of spiritual as well. Some of us have now and then differed in judgment, and differed earnestly,—as it was our right and privilege to do. But none of these differences have left the least trace of unkindness behind them, and I have often derived suggestions that were most valuable from opinions or arguments with which I could not fully coincide. Our meetings for Christian conference and prayer have not been always as large or as earnest as they should have been. But they have never failed to be held; and the brief remark, or the hesitating prayer, which came from the heart of some brother in the Church, has been to me often more stimulating in itself, or through the trains of thought it suggested, than a folio volume would have been. The glance of an eye suffused with tears at our

Communion has interpreted to me the appeals of the Cross, has manifested the secret of Christian experience, and has brought the Lord, to whom the tear was a tribute, more vividly before me than could pictures or statues. The penitence of a soul, pierced with the inmost sense of sin, has shown the hurt which only the grace of God can medicine; and the joy of one just converted to Christ has been more truly instructive and inspiring than any series of treatises or of lectures.

In a word, whatever I have been enabled to bring to you, of quickening counsel, of elevating and enlightening presentation of the truth, of the manifestation of the grace which is in Christ, of the revelation of the glory overhead,—that, I may freely confess tonight, that I have learned at first from you, or from your fellow-members here, more than from books, teachers, or schools. In ministering to you in the hour of your sorrow, I have touched through you the deepest sources of spiritual comfort. In wrestling with some of you, to lead you to Christ, or to bring you out afterward into a clearer and sweeter experience of the love, and light, and liberty of the Gospel, I have gained more wisdom and insight from you, when you knew it not, than I could possibly render back. In that energetic and unwearying zeal for all good works which some among you have signally shown, my own feebler faith and more languid enthusiasm has many times been bathed and refreshed. From the generous readiness with which you so often have responded to appeals for the furtherance of the truth, I have learned to trust more frankly and implicitly that central principle of Christian benevolence which is the source of all best deeds, and that supreme hold which the Gospel possesses on those who once have felt its power. And when, more than once, I have ministered to those whose eyes were closing on all scenes of Time, and have gone up with them, with clasped hands, almost unto the heavenly gates—until their grasp loosened from mine, to catch that of the angels who took my place,—it has been surely my shame and sin if I have not brought back from thence a conviction, a faith, a hope of glory, which have thereafter flashed as a light and burned as a flame through prayer and speech!

I thank you here for your ministry to me. Greater than mine to you it hath been. And often the thoughts which have moved you most have been but the echo of those which you, or others whom you loved, had stirred unknowing within my soul.

And I entreat the same ministry still, in the days, if it shall be the months or the years, which are to come. Especially I entreat it of those of you who have just entered the Church, led home to Christ in some degree through my imperfect ministrations. To you, my dear Friends,—whose hope is my joy, whose progress my prayer, and for whose welfare there is nothing I possess too precious to be given,—to you I may most appropriately repeat, what Paul said so earnestly to the recent converts at Thessalonica: "Now do we live, if *ye* stand fast in the Lord!"

The ministry of those who have been here before you—some of whom tarry with us still, while some are not, for God has called them—has been in the main very noble and helpful; with imperfections marking it, doubtless; with something of error, and something of sin, mingling entwined with its choicest activities; but still on the whole unusually full of faith, of freedom, of Christian courage, of love to the Master, and of consecrated zeal. Let your future ministry of spiritual life, to the Church, to your pastor, and to all whom the Church and its pastor affect, be one still nobler and more renewing!

Let the central flame of Christian love burn in your hearts with an undying constancy and pureness. Let your sweet charity, and patience, and peace, breathe as a fragrance throughout this enlarging society of believers. Let the sustaining and heavenly hope, which comes through Christ, impart its beauty to your character always, and shine with clear celestial lustre throughout your life. Let your self-devoted labors for others reach out to them, and bring both them and us a blessing. Take what of influence from the spheres unseen you here may meet, and make it felt throughout the circles which you affect. Seek first of all in yourselves, at all times, the richest, brightest, most abounding experience of all that which the Spirit of God will work, through the Gospel, in the hearts and minds of those who receive him; of all which study, prayer, and effort, beneficent action, and the wisest self-discipline, can bring to the soul through Christ its Lord; of all which God imparts in his grace to those whom he chooses for his own. And then let this be spontaneously revealed, in endurance and in action, in your life and on your lips, in all the circumstances in which you may be placed.

Then shall you be partakers on earth of the joys to be wholly known in Heaven! Then shall you walk, throughout these years which I trust stretch before you, as expectant not only, but inwardly assured,—yea, conscious already,—of the glory to come! Then shall you teach all those around you, and me among them, while here you tarry, of noblest themes, of highest attainments, of things above! And then shall your influence, outlasting your life, be still as vitally at work in this Church, through my words or through those of others, when you have ascended to your rest!

The eyes which I have seen hitherto, closing in death, with triumph in them,—they shine upon me still as I remember them! They shine to-day, unknown by you, on you through me! The voices that here have touched my heart, with their penitence or their praise,—they shall continue to touch yours, and those of others, as long as I here fulfil my ministry! The examples of fortitude, resignation, submission, or of a manly Christian resolve, a glowing zeal, a contagious beneficence, which I have here seen,—they are not lost; they are not silent. They are lifted from the pews. They are gathered here to-day from chamber and street, from counting-room and from grave-side. They find a voice always on my poor words. And they, and they chiefly, now give to those words whatever of worth or of weight they have.

Let your lives so speak, then, in like manner hereafter; and your example and spirit so testify; and your very death, irradiated from above, become the almoner, to those whom you leave, of spiritual life. So shall he who teaches you here in coming years, whoever he may be, be able to say to you, to the end of his ministry, as I say now to those into whose blessed fellowship in the Gospel you recently are incorporate, 'Now do we live, because ye are faithful!' And so, through Eternity, shall that vast, subtile, spiritual influence which emanates from you, continue to be felt, in souls hereafter born to God, while you rejoice before him in his glory!

Thanks to His Name for the present hope which fills our hearts, which shall then have expired in eternal fruition! Thanks to His Name for the kindness and grace which have brought us together, and have knit us through love in this fellowship of faith, of mutual helpfulness, and of a coming immortal joy! May no one, reckoned among us now, be wanting in the day when God maketh up his jewels! May no one who has confessed the Lord here—before the table crowned with the memorials of his sacrifice and cross—be left out from his Marriage Supper! But may we all, whose hearts have touched and quickened each other, amid these pleasant courts below, walk together in white, beneath the swell of saintly songs and seraph trumpets, when all the ransomed, of every land, are gathered by Christ in his resplendent heavenly city!

And unto Him who died, who lives, and through whom we may live forever, be all the praise! AMEN.

www.ingramcontent.com/pod-product-compliance
Lightning Source LLC
Chambersburg PA
CBHW031551110426
42739CB00039B/1018